CRAFT ATTACK!

PAPER CRAFTS

Annalees Lim

W
FRANKLIN WATTS
LONDON • SYDNEY

First published in 2014 by Franklin Watts

Copyright © 2014 Arcturus Publishing Limited

Franklin Watts
338 Euston Road
London NW1 3BH

Franklin Watts Australia
Level 17/207 Kent Street, Sydney NSW 2000

Produced by Arcturus Publishing Limited,
26/27 Bickels Yard, 151–153 Bermondsey Street, London SE1 3HA

Editors: Joe Harris and Sara Gerlings
Design: Elaine Wilkinson
Cover design: Elaine Wilkinson
Photography: Simon Pask

A CIP catalogue record for this book is available from the British Library.

Dewey Decimal Classification Number 745.5'4
ISBN 978 1 4451 2934 1

Printed in China

Franklin Watts is a division of Hachette Children's Books, an Hachette UK company.

www.hachette.co.uk

SL003837UK
Supplier 03, Date 0114, Print Run 3034

CONTENTS

GETTING CRAFTY WITH PAPER

What do you think when you see a piece of paper? Do you just see a blank surface for you to write on? Well, look again. In this book you will discover that paper can be the perfect material for cool craft projects.

Paper, Paper, Everywhere!

You don't have to rush out to buy a new pack of coloured paper to make the projects in this book. Just look around you and think about how you could re-use old wrapping paper, magazines or even paper plates left over from a birthday party.

Other Bits and Bobs

Once you've found some paper, you can hunt around for fun materials to make your projects extra special. Use glitter or brightly coloured ribbons to make your creations sparkle and stand out. Cut up spare photographs (remembering to ask an adult first!) to give a project the personal touch.

Keep It Clean!

If you are painting or using a messy technique, make sure you cover the surface you are working on with newspaper or a piece of plastic.

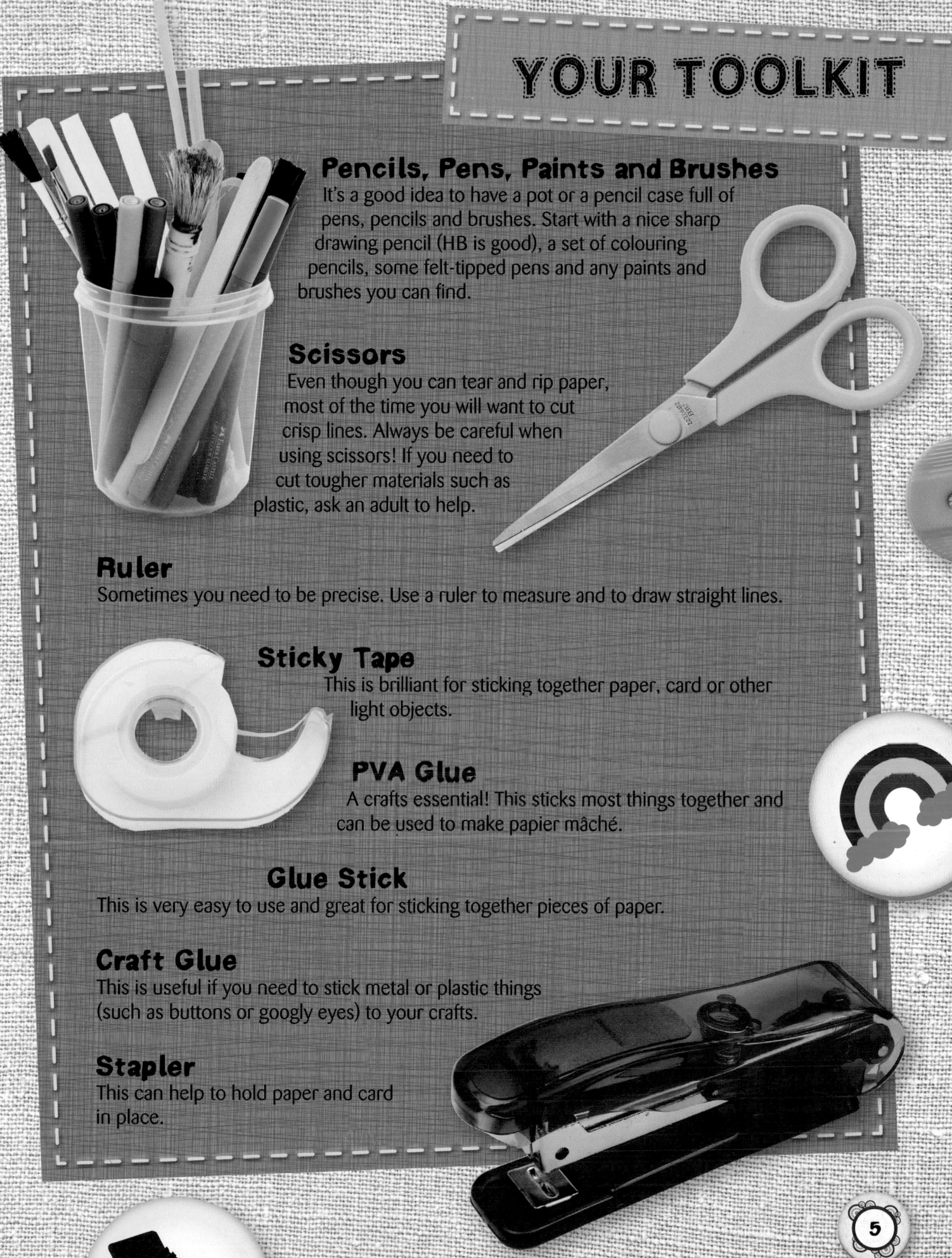

Pencils, Pens, Paints and Brushes

It's a good idea to have a pot or a pencil case full of pens, pencils and brushes. Start with a nice sharp drawing pencil (HB is good), a set of colouring pencils, some felt-tipped pens and any paints and brushes you can find.

Scissors

Even though you can tear and rip paper, most of the time you will want to cut crisp lines. Always be careful when using scissors! If you need to cut tougher materials such as plastic, ask an adult to help.

Ruler

Sometimes you need to be precise. Use a ruler to measure and to draw straight lines.

Sticky Tape

This is brilliant for sticking together paper, card or other light objects.

PVA Glue

A crafts essential! This sticks most things together and can be used to make papier mâché.

Glue Stick

This is very easy to use and great for sticking together pieces of paper.

Craft Glue

This is useful if you need to stick metal or plastic things (such as buttons or googly eyes) to your crafts.

Stapler

This can help to hold paper and card in place.

CUBE PUZZLE

Decorate your paper boxes with a pattern, then jumble them up. How quickly can you put them back together in the right order?

You will need:

1 Measure a 5 x 5 cm (2 in x 2 in) square of card. This is your template. Use scissors to cut it out, then draw around the square six times on a piece of paper to make a 'T' shape.

2 Use your scissors to cut out the 'T' shape and then fold along each line, pressing firmly to make a crisp fold.

3 Fold the sides of the 'T' up to make a cube. Fix everything in place using sticky tape. Make another eight cubes, so that there are nine cubes in total.

4 Tracing around your template again, draw a large square made up of nine smaller squares. Cut out circles of coloured card and glue them on in a pattern. Each circle should overlap at least two squares.

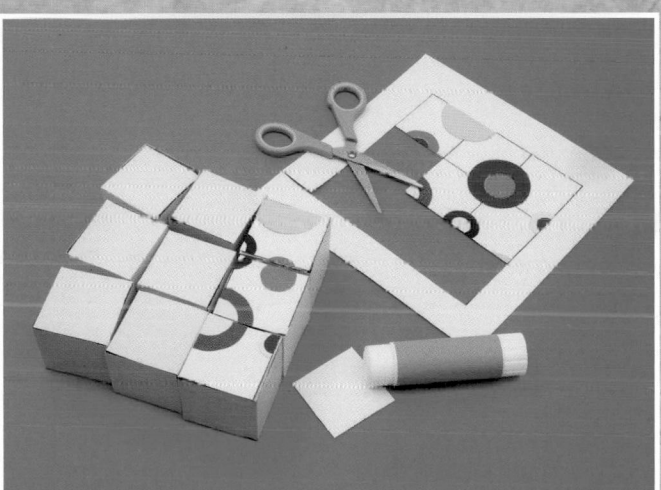

5 One by one, cut out the patterned squares and stick them onto the face of your cubes using a glue stick. If you would like to make the puzzle extra hard, you could repeat steps 4 and 5 so that your cubes have part of a different pattern on each side.

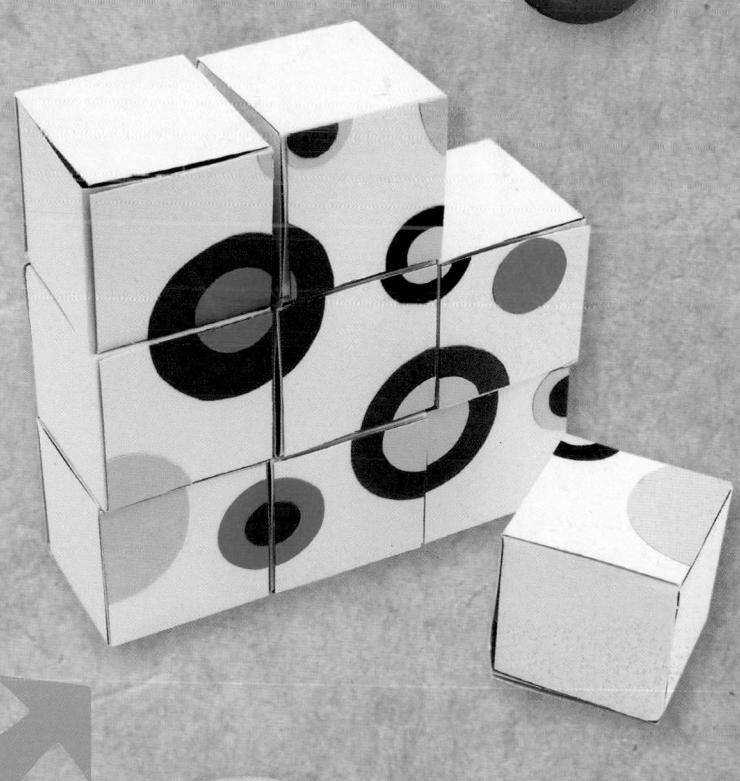

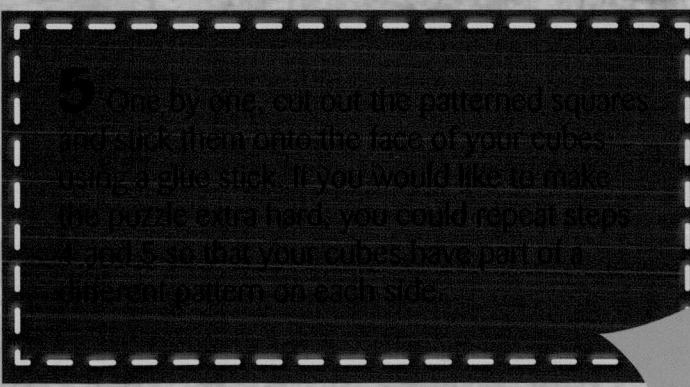

POP-UP PAINTING

Paintings usually lie flat against the canvas. But this craft project will make your artwork leap out into the third dimension!

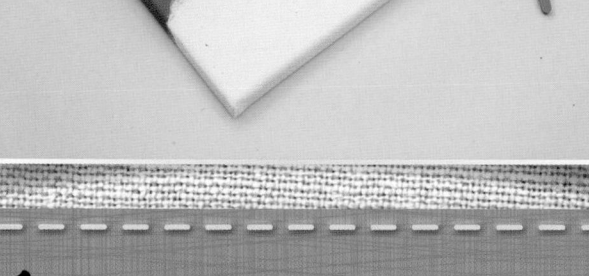

1 With a brush, paint your canvas in a bright colour using acrylic paints. Leave to dry.

2 Fold a piece of paper in half, and then in half again. Draw a large butterfly shape and a small butterfly shape onto one side and cut out using your scissors. This will make eight butterflies in total.

3 Fold a piece of green paper in half and half again. Draw some leaf shapes onto it and cut them out. Fold each butterfly and leaf in half so that it looks like the butterflies are fluttering and the leaves are shaped like real leaves.

4 Start building up your canvas by gluing the leaves onto the canvas. Only glue down the folded edge so that the paper stands out from the canvas.

PAPER PLANETS

This papier mâché project uses tissue paper instead of ordinary paper. It will create such an eye-catching display that you will want to cover your whole room with these gorgeous globes.

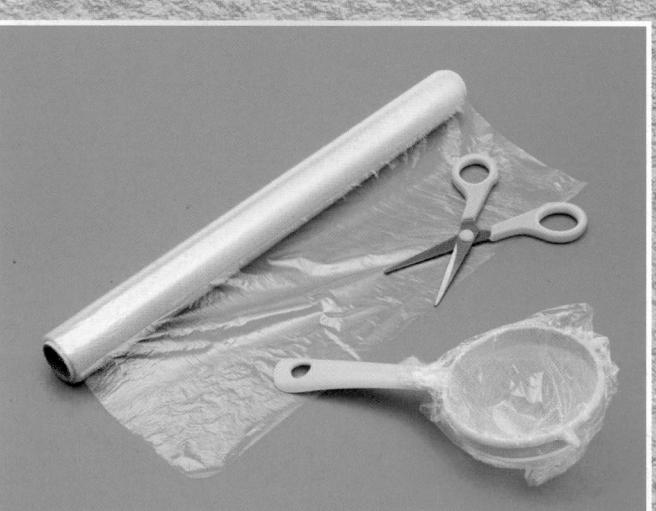

1 Cut out two pieces of cling film and use them to line the insides of your bowls or sieves.

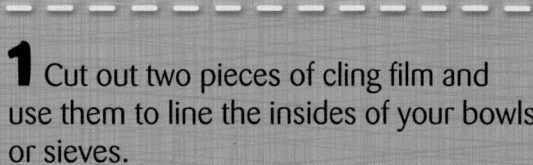

2 Rip the tissue paper into small pieces. Cover the inside of each bowl or sieve with a thin layer of PVA glue and tissue paper.

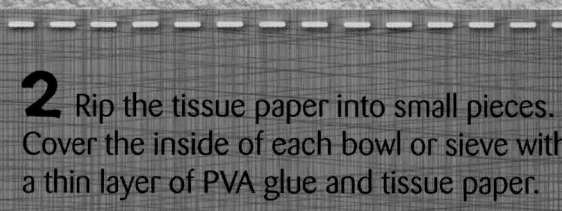

3 Repeat until you have created three layers of glue and tissue paper. Leave to dry.

4 Carefully remove the tissue paper shapes from the bowls and cling film. These will be the two halves of your globe. Sandwich a length of string between the two halves. Then stick them together using PVA glue and more tissue paper to cover the join. Leave to dry.

PAPER PULP MONSTERS

Paper pulp is great, messy fun. You can shape and mould the pulp into crazy shapes and creatures... such as these monsters!

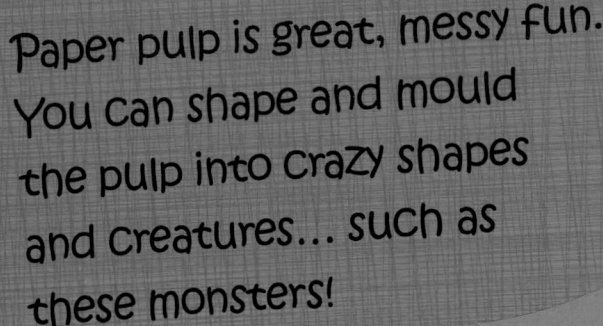

1 Half-fill a plastic pot with water. Tear some tissue paper into small pieces and put it in the pot. Leave to soak for a few hours.

2 Remove the tissue paper and squeeze out the excess water. Empty any water from the pot and put the tissue back inside.

3 Pour in some PVA glue and mix together well with the stirrer to make the paper pulp.

4 Cover your work surface with a plastic sheet. Mould the paper pulp mixture into the shape of a monster. Then make some more in other colours!

5 Press googly eyes onto your monsters and leave them to dry in a warm place.

MAKE YOUR OWN NOTEBOOK

Keep your notes, scribbles and doodles in one place with this handy, handmade hardback book.

1 Fold the 10 pieces of A4 paper in half and secure them in place by using one staple in the middle of the folded edge.

2 Cover one side of the stiff card with wrapping paper. Fold the paper around the edges of the card, and stick it down with tape.

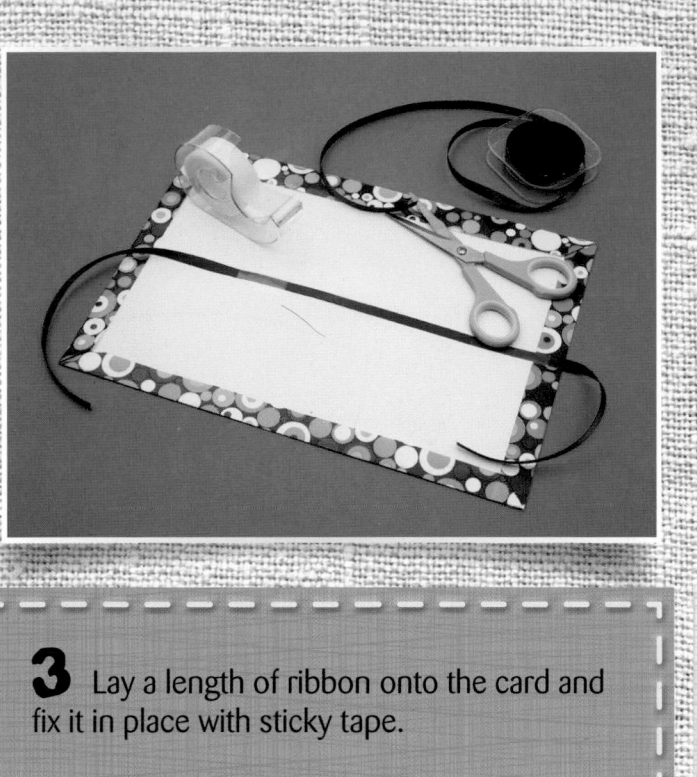

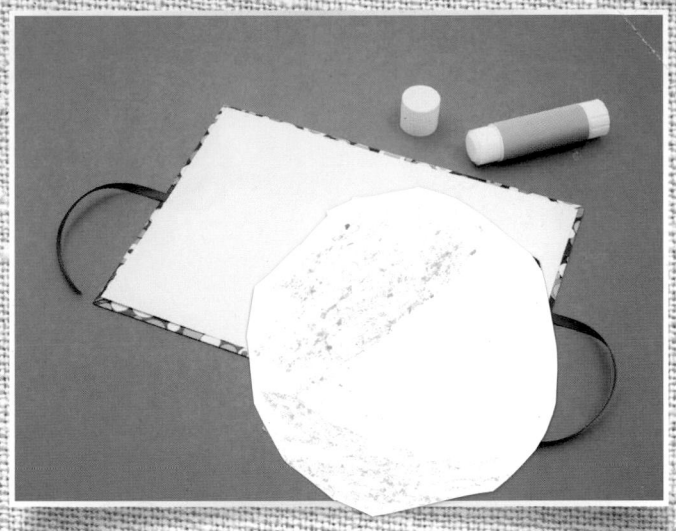

3 Lay a length of ribbon onto the card and fix it in place with sticky tape.

4 Cover the ribbon with a piece of coloured paper that is slightly smaller than the card and fix it in place with a glue stick.

5 Fold the card in half and sandwich the paper pages inside. Secure everything in place using two staples at the top and bottom of the spine.

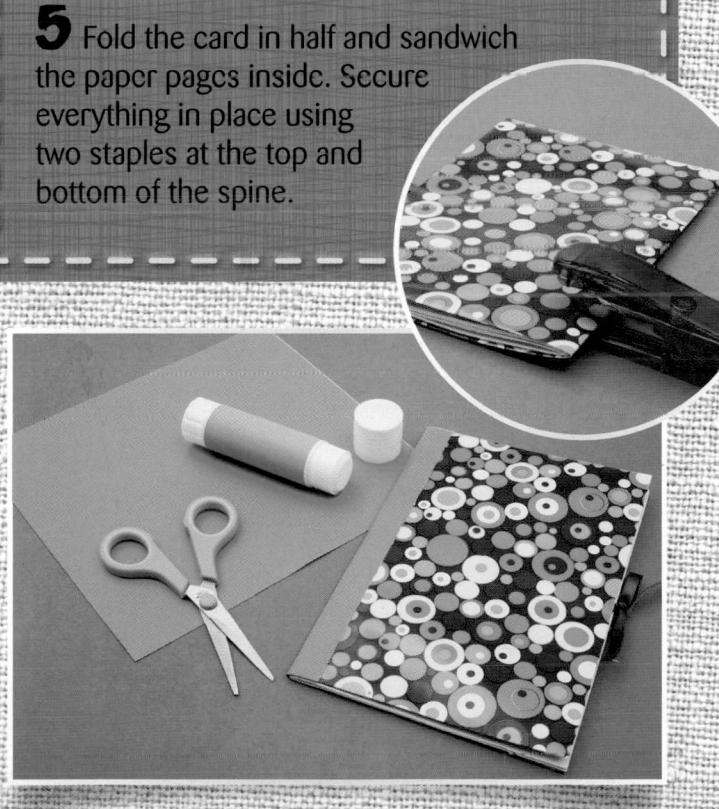

SECRET SEASHELL STORAGE BOX

This lovely seashell-shaped box is perfect for displaying sparkly jewellery. You could also use it to show off your collection of real seashells to remind you of a seaside holiday!

You will need
- Paper plates
- Card
- Metallic paint
- Paintbrushes
- Tissue paper
- Stapler
- Scissors
- Black marker pen
- Masking tape

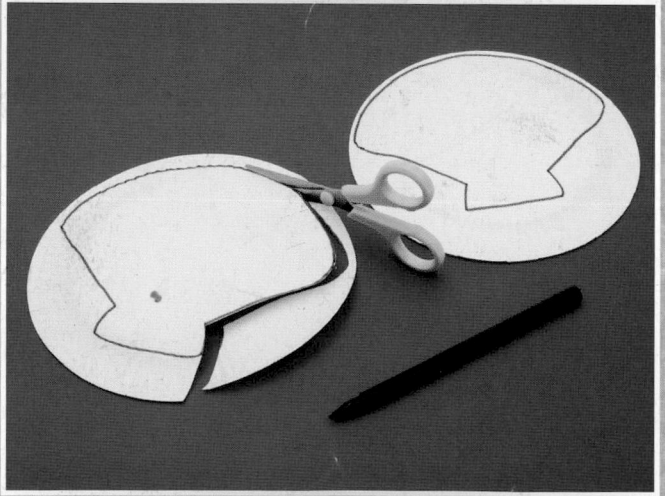

1 Draw a shell shape onto two paper plates using your marker pen, then cut them out with scissors.

2 Paint both sides using your brushes and the metallic paint. Leave to dry.

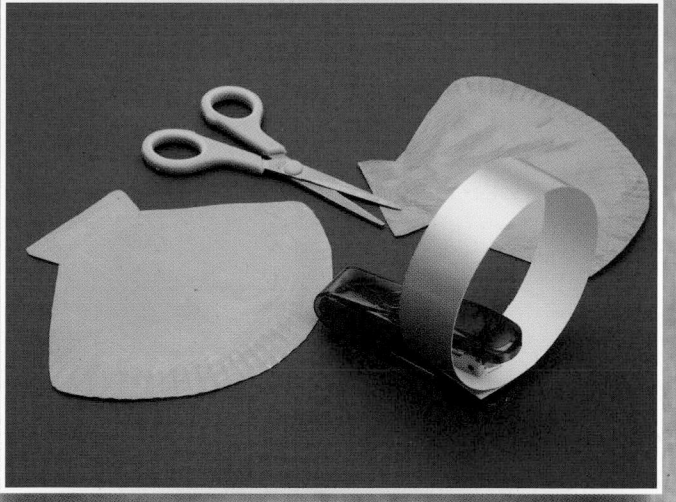

3 Cut a 3-cm (1-in) thick strip of card, and bend it into a circle. It must be small enough to fit inside the paper shell. Staple it in place and paint it the same colour as the shell.

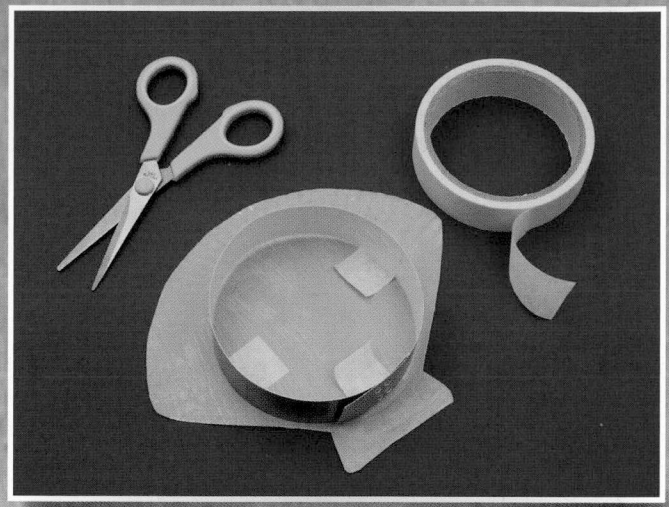

4 Fix the card circle to one of the paper plate shells using strips of masking tape.

5 Make a hinge by folding a rectangle-shaped piece of card. Stick one side to the card circle as shown, and then glue on the seashell lid.

6 Line the inside with tissue paper.

17

3-D PHOTO ART

Taking photographs is a good way to keep a record of all the fun times you've had. By printing multiple copies of the same photo, you can make a 3-D découpage photo to display. It will look like the picture is leaping out at you!

You will need

4 copies of the same photograph
Scissors
Sticky foam pads
Card
Glue stick

1 Cut a piece of card to the same size as your photographs. Glue one of the photographs onto the card using a glue stick.

2 Take another copy of the photograph and cut out the whole foreground, using scissors. Then, take the third copy of the photograph and cut out a smaller part of the foreground.

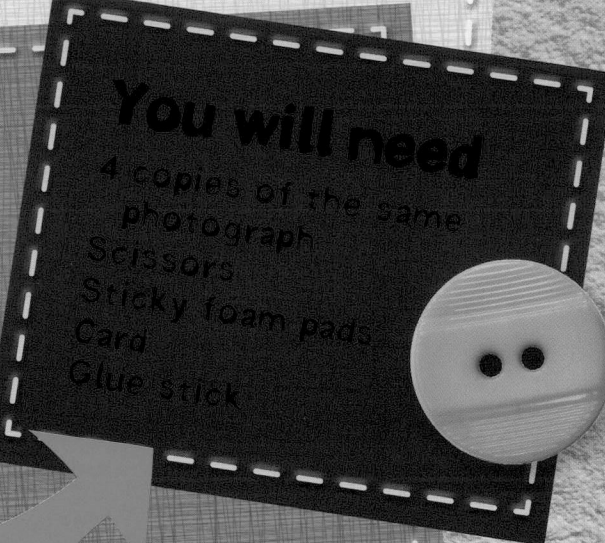

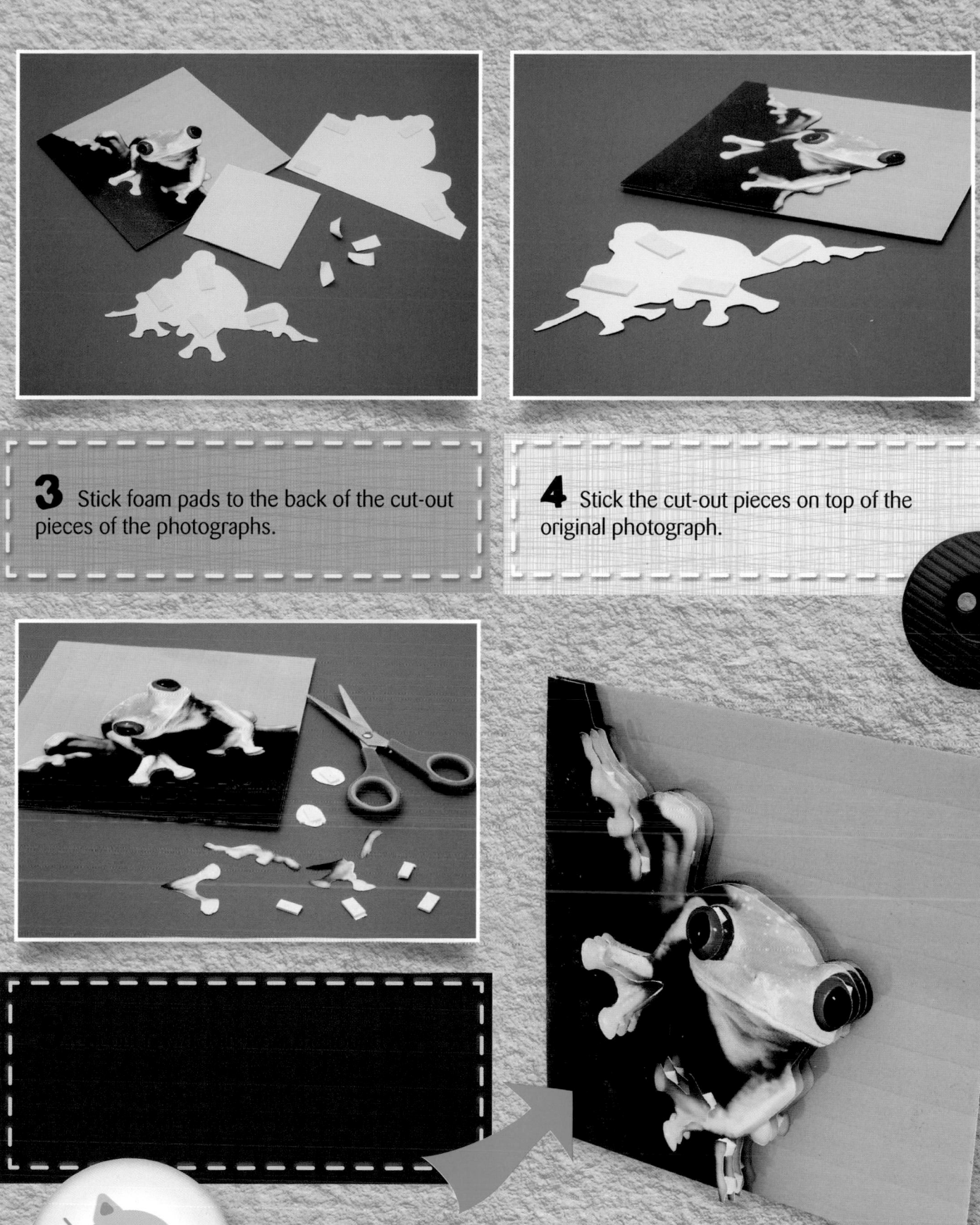

3 Stick foam pads to the back of the cut-out pieces of the photographs.

4 Stick the cut-out pieces on top of the original photograph.

19

QUILLING CARDS

Quilling is a way of folding or curling paper to create amazing patterns. These cards are pretty to look at and easy to make. All you need is a steady hand!

You will need
Coloured paper
A shredder or scissors
Card
Glue stick
Pen

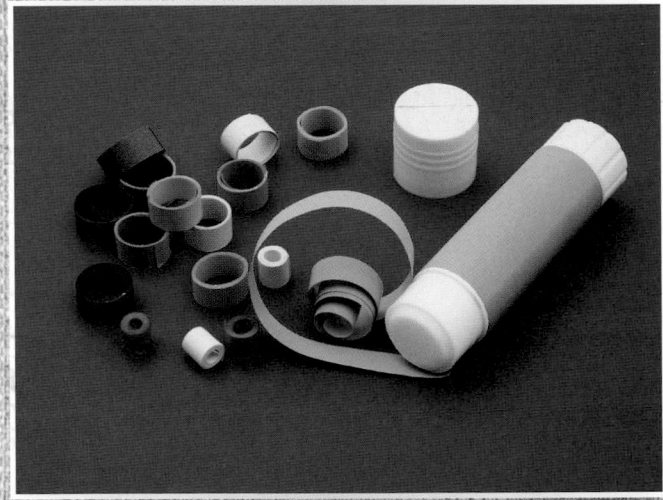

1 Use a shredder to cut the coloured paper into strips. If you don't have a shredder you can always cut it by hand using scissors, but make sure the strips are as even as possible.

2 Coil each strip of paper into a tight circle and fix it in place using a glue stick.

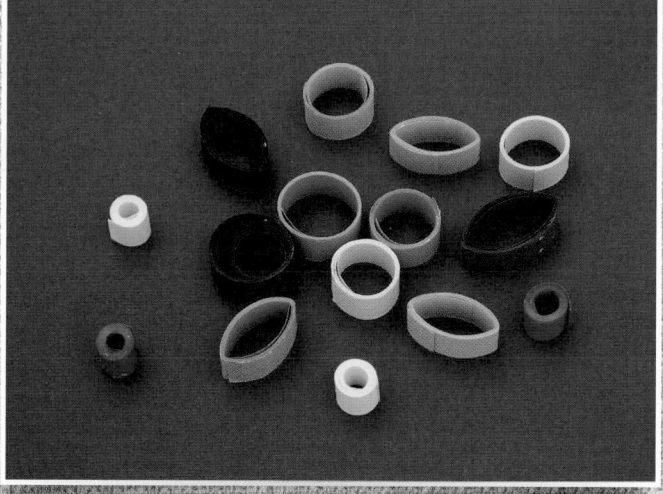

3 Make some of the circles big and some of them small. Squash some of the circles so that they turn into ellipse shapes.

4 Fold a piece of card in two. Using a pen, draw a big star shape on one side.

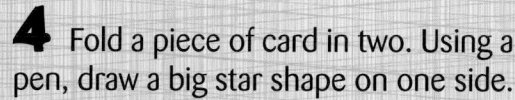

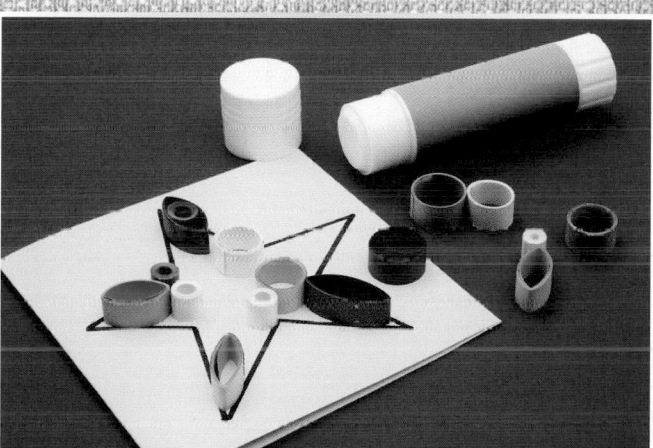

5 Cover the inside of the star shape with some glue stick and press the shapes into the glue. Fill the whole shape with the quilled coils of paper. Leave to dry.

GIANT CRAYONS

These crazy crayons make for a fun bedroom decoration. They look just like the real thing — only 10 times bigger!

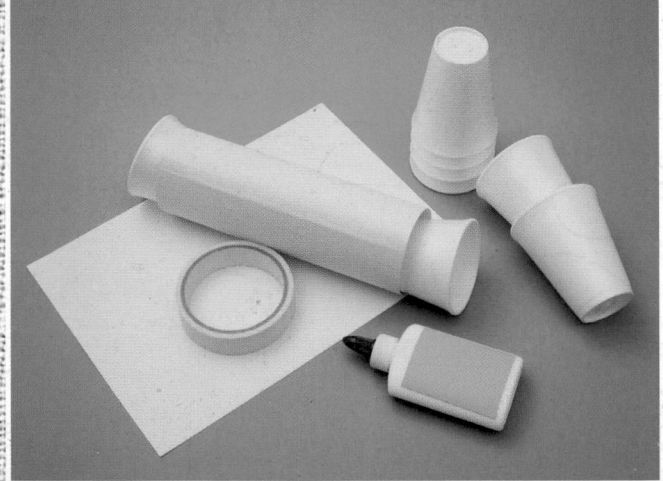

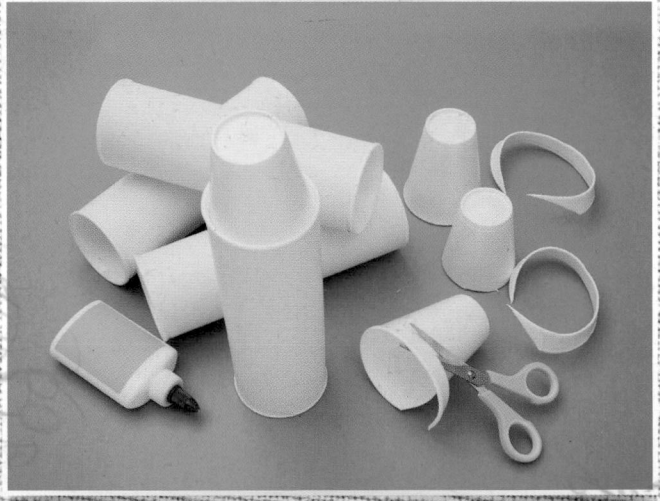

1 Roll a piece of paper into a tube just big enough to fit a polystyrene cup inside. Hold the tube together with masking tape.

2 Use scissors to cut off the rim of a cup. Stick it to the top of the tube with glue to make the crayon. Then make three more!

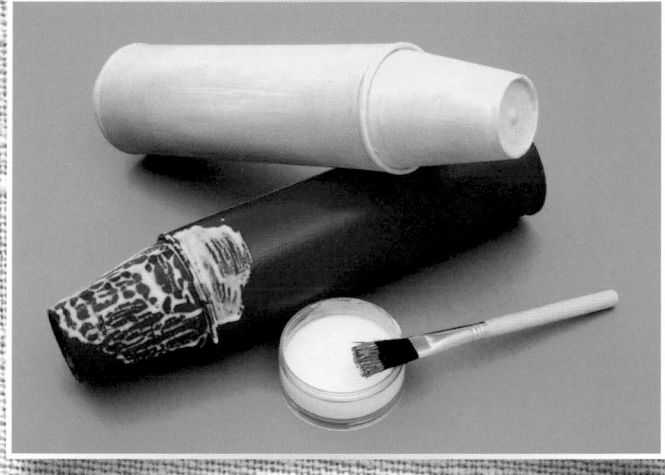

3 Paint each giant crayon in a bright colour with acrylic paints and leave to dry.

4 Give each crayon a coat of PVA glue. It will dry see-through and make your crayon look waxy and shiny.

5 With a marker, draw details onto pieces of paper that match the colours of the crayons.

6 Stick the pieces of paper onto the crayons and fix them in place with sticky tape.

23

PAPER GLOBE LAMPSHADE

Brighten up your room by decorating a plain paper globe lampshade with cute cartoon pictures.

You will need:

1 Draw a design onto a piece of paper. This pattern will be repeated around your lampshade three times.

2 Trace your design three times onto pieces of tissue paper. Copy different elements onto different coloured paper.

3 Cut all your pieces out using scissors and arrange them in order so they match your design.

4 Paint a thin layer of PVA glue onto the whole of the lampshade. Start sticking on your tissue paper designs, one piece at a time.

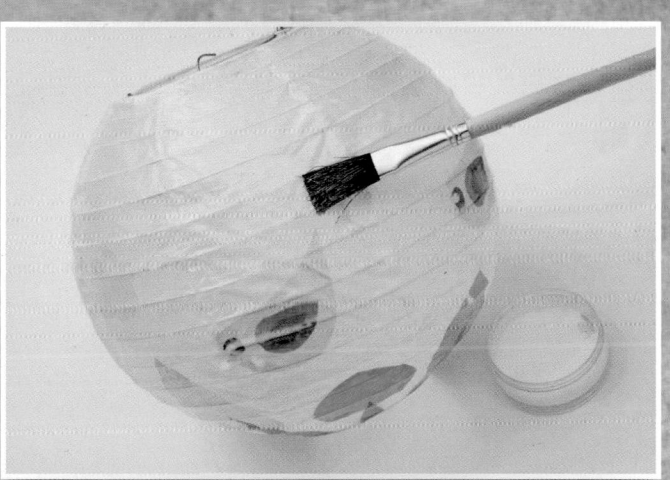

PAPER CUP DISCO BALL

Disco balls are covered in mirrors that reflect light around a nightclub. This decoration can do the same for your bedroom! Watch as the light bounces around when the sun hits it.

1 Cut the bottoms off 18 paper cups.

2 Fix together a ring of eight paper cup tops, using a stapler.

3 Staple three more cups together in a line and then staple them to opposite cups in the ring to make a kind of bridge.

4 Staple two more cups to join the middle cup of the bridge and the middle cup on each side of the ring. Repeat steps 3 and 4 on the other side so that you make a complete globe.

6 Tie a piece of string to the top of your disco ball so you can hang it up.

ENVELOPES AND NOTEPAPER

Personalised stationery looks really cool. People will love to receive customised letters from you! They'll look even better in handmade envelopes.

1 Cut a piece of wrapping paper into a square 20 cm x 20 cm (8 in x 8 in). Cut around three of the edges to make them round. Snip a triangle off the other corner.

2 Fold the flat corner into the middle on the other side of the paper. Press it firmly to make a crisp crease.

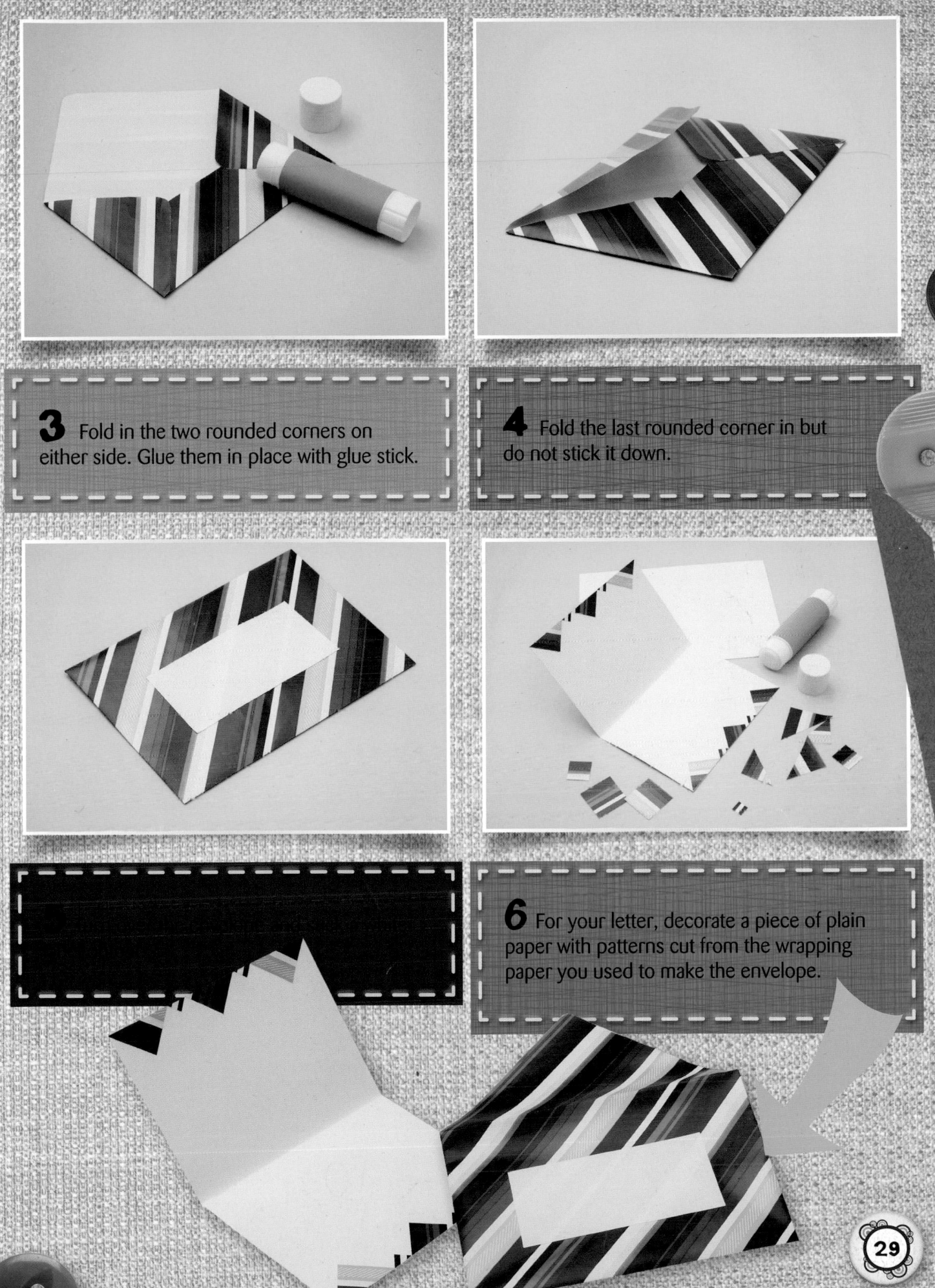

3 Fold in the two rounded corners on either side. Glue them in place with glue stick.

4 Fold the last rounded corner in but do not stick it down.

6 For your letter, decorate a piece of plain paper with patterns cut from the wrapping paper you used to make the envelope.

29

PAPER BOUQUET

The art of making paper flowers is centuries old and is still popular today. Give your bouquet to a teacher to say thank you, or to a friend or family member as a gift.

1 Put a strip of double-sided sticky tape along both sides of the long edge of the coloured paper. Do not remove the paper backing from the tape yet!

2 Fold the paper in half lengthways so that the two strips of tape meet. Then fold it in half widthways.

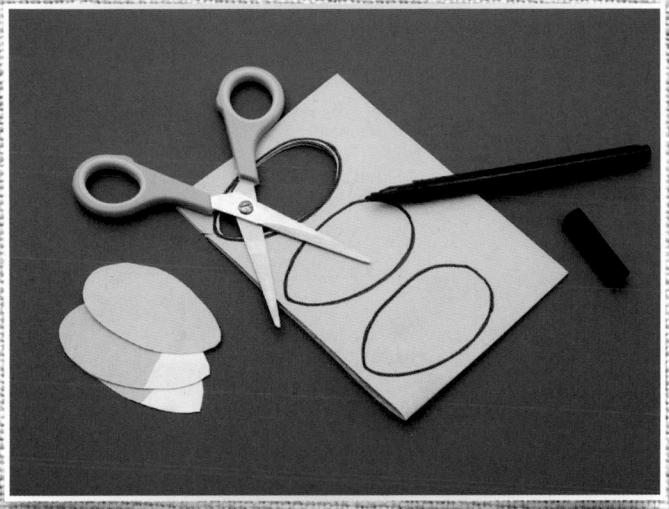

3 Draw three petal shapes onto the paper, making sure that one end of each petal is over the sticky tape. Cut them out with scissors.

4 Peel off the paper from the tape on one petal. Stick the petal around the top of a green garden cane.

5 Repeat this, going around the cane until you have used all the petals.

6 Repeat steps 1–5 with different-coloured paper until you have enough flower stems to make a bouquet! Peel back the petals to make the flowers look like they are in bloom.

31

GLOSSARY

acetate A transparent sheet of plastic.

customise To make something in a special way to suit a particular person.

element Part of an object.

ellipse A shape like a squashed circle.

polystyrene A type of plastic, which can be either stiff or a kind of foamy material.

quilling A craft technique where paper or fabric is layered and folded to make patterns.

shredder A machine for cutting paper into strips.

FURTHER READING

365 Things to do with Paper and Cardboard by Fiona Watt (Usborne, 2011)
Big Book of Papercraft by Fiona Watt (Usborne, 2009)
Paper Play: Roll it. Rip it. Fold it. Snip it! by Lydia Crook (Ivy Press, 2013)
Paper, Scissors, Glue by Polly Wreford (Ryland Peters & Small, 2010)

WEBSITES

www.bbc.co.uk/cbbc/thingstodo/by/type/createandmake
Crafts from popular television programmes.
www.busybeekidscrafts.com/Paper-Crafts-for-Kids.html
Animal themed papercrafts.
kids.nationalgeographic.co.uk/kids/activities/crafts/
Crafts inspired by nature.

INDEX

SERIES CONTENTS

Jewellery Crafts

Make Your Own Jewellery • Pendant Necklace • Lucky Rabbit Earrings • Brilliant Bead Bracelet • Knotted Bracelet • Cool Collar Necklace • Fabric Flower Ring • Friends Forever Necklaces • Sew Easy Felt Brooch • Funky Toy Hair Clips • Jewelled Cuff • Puzzle Piece Hair Comb • Button Bag Charm • Jewellery Tree

Nature Crafts

Going Wild with Nature Crafts • Woodland Photo Frame • Painted Pebble Plant Pot • Butterfly Bunting • Sand Art • Shell Creature Fridge Magnets • Pressed Flower Coasters • Leafy Bird Mobile • Seed Mosaic • Japanese Blossom Tree • Pebble Zoo • Brilliant Bird Box • Pine Cone Field Mouse • Lavender Hand Warmers

Paper Crafts

Getting Crafty with Paper • Cube Puzzle • Pop-Up Painting • Paper Planets • Paper Pulp Monsters • Make Your Own Notebook • Secret Seashell Storage Box • 3-D Photo Art • Quilling Cards • Giant Crayons • Paper Globe Lampshade • Paper Cup Disco Ball • Envelopes and Notepaper • Paper Bouquet

Printing Crafts

Perfect Printing • Apple Print Canvas Bag • Block Printed Cards • One-Off Portrait Print • Funky Pattern Prints • Stencil Art Plant Pot • Clay Printing • Roller Print Folders • Cling Film Wrapping Paper • Button Print Trainers • Easy Screen Prints • Spotty Painted Mugs • Bubble Print T-Shirt • Sandpaper Printing

Recycling Crafts

Crafty Recycling • Jam Jar Lanterns • Bottle Tops in Bloom • Funny Face Vase • Stackable Rocket Boxes • Beach Hut Pen Pots • Bedroom Pinboard • Water Bottle Bracelets • Scrap Paper Daisy Chain • Peacock Bookends • Sunny Days Clock • Starry Sky Mail Mobile • CD Case Photo Frame • Plastic Bag Weaving

Textile Crafts

Terrific Textiles • Cute Sock Owls • Rock Star Rag Doll • Toadstool Doorstop • Funky Felt Friend • Cocoa Cosy • Totally Brilliant Tote • Awesome Accessories • Jean Genius Desk Mascot • Secret Diary Cover • Mini Bag Organizer • Cupcake Pincushion • Knitted Phone Case